Follow your Dreams!

Jenni Fer

Additional Praise for
HOW TO HAVE A SUCCESSFUL
BRIDAL SHOWER A TO Z

"This book is a must-read for every bride-to-be and her friends. How clever Jerri is to incorporate all of these original ideas into an A to Z format. It makes the book amazingly helpful and creative— a true resource guide!"

—Michelle Purple, Executive Producer, The Sinner

"Who wouldn't want an EMMY-winning producer and writer giving personal advice about how to produce the bridal shower of a lifetime! This book lives up to its name. I am tasked with putting on my 1st bridal shower and have gone from completely intimidated to here I come! Jerri Sher is apparently as much a loving mom who has gone to the ends of the earth for her daughters as she is an industry name. She leaves no stone unturned in a highly creative, exceedingly detailed, easily attainable blueprint for bridal showers -- based on her own experiences. There are literally 1000's of amazing ideas in here. Choose one or choose a dozen and one for yourself (I'm having trouble deciding), and get this book for all the brides, moms, sisters, grandmothers, cousins, and friends of brides in your orbit. I just did!"

—Beth Herman, Washington Post Contributor, Novelist, Journalist & Coauthor of HEALTHY STABLES by DESIGN

HOW TO HAVE
A SUCCESSFUL
bridal shower

HOW TO HAVE
A SUCCESSFUL
bridal shower

With More Than **500 Creative** Ideas

JERRI SHER

REDWOOD PUBLISHING, LLC

ISBN eBook: 978-0-692-76973-7
ISBN Paperback: 978-1-947341-10-4

Cover Design: Mihaela Cocea

For Alan, Amy and Heather, and my dear family and friends, who I have entertained in order to bring joy, laughter and love into your lives—through parties!

Contents

*A*round the time that a girl/guy gets engaged everyone will ask…when is the shower?

*B*ecause everyone wants to celebrate this happy occasion with friends and relatives…you need to plan a party!

*C*onsidering the fact that many brides do not live in the city in which they were born…there may be more than one party.

*D*epending on where the groom's family lives, there may be another celebration or two…and more presents!

*E*ngagement parties are often hosted by the future in-laws… commonly known in Jewish circles as the mishpacha. But in any faith or nationality, it means planning!

*F*riends in the bridal party usually plan something for the bride as well…and that means more gifts!

*G*raphic designs on the following pages will inspire you to plan a great party…with a great invitation.

*H*ire help for the kitchen if you are not catering the affair or booking a restaurant…you deserve to enjoy the day.

*I*nvitations set the tone and inspire enthusiasm the minute your guest opens the envelope…or box (with a gift).

*J*uggling the guest list will be one of your biggest challenges; when in doubt, invite…more gifts for the bride!

*K*eep accurate lists (addresses, emails, and RSVPs)… for the bride's thank you notes.

*L*earn important names in advance…especially the guest of honor's mother, sister, grandmother, and other family members.

*M*ail invitations six to eight weeks in advance…guests need notice as everyone's calendar gets so booked up these days.

*N*ail down your form of entertainment early…so that you have an exciting theme.

*O*pen bridal shower games long before the event and read the instructions…so the party runs smoothly.

*P*eruse interesting stores or websites for prizes and favors for your guests…more specifics throughout the book.

*Q*uestion the groom about the courtship for a newlywed-type game…details to follow.

*R*elax prior to the party with a bubble bath and great music...you deserve a heavenly time-out.

*S*ave all of your notes on details of the event...everyone will call you for advice (consider this a compliment).

*T*hink...fun...fantasy...laughter...forget boring and same old, same old.

*U*nique and unusual is okay...by reading this book you will now be creative, yes, your party can be the first!

*V*ary the following menus, themes, games, party titles, names, invitations, and centerpieces...feel free to mix and match everything and anything you read on the following pages.

*W*hether you live in the North, South, East or West...there is an appropriate party for you.

*X*pensive (thousands of $$$) or strictly low budget makes no difference...you will find your comfort zone and adjust accordingly.

*Y*outh (10-year-olds) and elderly (95-year-old great-grandmothers) will have a great time together... even if they don't know one another.

Zip along now from A through Z for pre-wedding events and / or birthday celebrations including brunches, cocktail parties, bachelorette weekends, Barbie-Qs, luncheons, dinners, and showers of all kinds. Enjoy the adventurous process choosing from hundreds of titles and themes (with your name!) on the following pages.

1
"A" Parties

Afternoon Tea with Amy

Alice in Bridal Land

Adorn Arielle with Gifts

Announcing Anita's Wedding

ADVICE FOR ALYSSA

Andrea Admits Her Love

Accessories for Alicia's Shower

Around the Fireplace with Allison

An Album for Ann

Ask Amanda Anything About Love

Angels Dance Around Angela

Ashley's Tea Party

Annette Awakens Absolutely in Love

Advice Cards for Alexis

An Aura Around Amelia—She's In Love!

Autumn Exudes

ADORING AERIN

Afternoon Tea with Amy

The beauty of this shower is that you may entertain your guests anywhere and the party will still be a success. A cozy living room in a house is perfectly fine for this type of event—or a decadent, rented castle. Collecting unusual china teacups and different patterns is one of the highlights of a tea. Mix and match dishes with friends and relatives even if you have to borrow extra place settings. The variety will be worth it.

Arrange a variety of exotic teas including herbal and caffeine with little dishes of honey, lemon, and sugar in various dishes. It is always a good idea to have coffee and hot chocolate (with whipped cream—more decadent!) on hand for the sweet tooth crowd. Some borrowed, interesting teapots will add to the exotic décor. Speaking of exotic, you may want to have a little brandy and liquor that may be added to the hot drinks.

Cookies (sugar; chocolate chip; peanut butter) and scones (blueberry; strawberry; chocolate) may be purchased, to save time and effort, at places such as Dunkin' Donuts—they are fresh, light, and delicious. Cakes (chocolate; poppy seed; angel food; carrot) and a delectable cheesecake (recipe to follow), are always coveted. Fancy fruits (strawberries; honeydew; cantaloupe; apples; pineapple; grapes; kiwis) cut up and displayed in a pineapple shell are all that is necessary for an afternoon tea. You might want to add ice cream balls that you have molded and shaped beforehand (maybe into heart shapes). A sundae bar with various chopped candy bars, nuts, and marshmallows brings some fun and flavor to the party as well. For the protein aficionados, a cheese board display will do the trick.

Advice cards may be created on index cards and sent out with your invitations. Each guest will be instructed to write some advice about health, love, foods, vacations, exercise, or clothes to bring to the party. The hostess will read the cards and ask the bride to guess who wrote the advice—or if it was a married lady or a single woman. Take a picture of each guest with the bride. Then after the pictures are printed, make a digital album or print a photo book for the guest of honor with the photos. Place each advice card next to the appropriate photo in the album. This makes a meaningful presentation that the bride will love!

Now for the recipe.

Cheese Cake
From Frau Reidling, Dossenheim, Germany 1970

Ingredients:
Pie Crust
    1½ cups flour
    1 egg
    ½ pound unsalted margarine
    ⅓ to ½ cup sugar
    1 lemon rind, grated
Filling
    1⅓ cups sugar
    1 cup sweet cream
    8 eggs
    2 tablespoons flour
    1½ pounds cottage cheese

Early in the day:

1. Mix all of the piecrust ingredients together until smooth and press into pie plate. Set aside.

2. Mix filling ingredients together then pour into piecrust.

3. Bake at 325°F for 70 to 90 minutes.

4. Use a toothpick to test for doneness. A perfectly successful dessert that will be the hit of the party. No one makes cheesecake better than Frau Reidling from the authentic little village outside of Heidelberg, Germany. We were lucky enough to live there for one year and learn all of her delicious recipes. With superb delectables such as this, everyone will be raving about your tea.

INVITATION: It's always a good idea to send something fun with your invitation. For this party, a tea bag is ideal. Or choose a theme with a huge floppy hat and have the information printed on the shape of a summer hat. You could also encourage all of your guests to wear a hat.

Some of the other titles in the "A" category above may be interchanged easily. For instance, **Advice Cards for Alexis** would be appropriate since the advice cards will be part of the entertainment. An Album for Ann is also fine since the photo album will be presented with all of the cards and pictures. If the tea is going to be at a home, restaurant, or castle with a fireplace, Around the Fireplace with Allison may be selected.

Of course, Ashley's Tea Party is a natural. If you like the theme *Accessories for Alicia's Shower*, plan exactly the same tea party but in the invitation (with this title) ask guests to bring the bride a fabulous accessory. Since the story of *Alice in Wonderland* was about a tea party, **Alice in Bridal Land** may also be adapted quite successfully. You will see throughout the following pages that you may mix and match names and ideas very simply. It also helps to use different fonts on your invitation. Take some hints from the fonts that are in this book. You are creating a mood, a feeling, a sensation of excitement and intrigue. Don't hold back!

If you decide to choose *Adorn Arielle with Gifts*, you can use the same tea party but in the invitation add the little confetti of tiny colored gift boxes that you can buy at any party favor store. For *Ask Amanda Anything About Love* the advice cards will come in handy, and for the confetti you can use question marks and hearts. If you like the sound of *Annette Awakens Absolutely in Love*, feel free to have the guests bring something for the bedroom such as a very fancy pillow.

It has been said that angels dance above flowers. For your tea party you might want to have little vases of various flowers all around the rooms. Send your invitation titled *Angels Dance Around Angela* and ask the guests at the party to guess why the name of the party was chosen and what it has to do with the decorations in the room. Have a nice prize for the winner or winners. Roses would be perfect!

2
"B" Parties

Barbara's Bridal Barbie-Q

Brenda's Bachelorette Weekend

Brunch for Betty

Bestow Gifts on Betsy

Beth's Bridal Registry

Because Brittany Will Be a Bride

Bathing Beauty Bernadette

BRING A GIFT FOR BEVERLY

Bridal Bingo is the Best at Bonny's Shower

Bernice's Bridal Shower Will Beat Her Birthday

BUY A GIFT AT THE BOUTIQUE FOR BROOKE

Bring Best Wishes for Blossom

Barbara's Bridal Barbie-Q

At the Barbie-Q it might be fun to use Barbie dolls as centerpieces for a retro décor. One table might be the iconic doll in a wedding dress, one might be in a bathrobe getting ready for the big event, another dressed in the outfit for the next day going off for the honeymoon, and one in a bathing suit ready for the beach. If the fiancée's name happens to be Ken, you could use the Ken doll as well. The guests will really get a kick out of that!

Whether you are having a party at home or at the country club, the menu may be similar. Barbecued chicken (for the health nuts), ribs, corn on the cob, hot dogs, hamburgers, tossed salad, pasta salad, and baked beans are all good choices (and chips of course). Tropical drinks like frozen strawberry daiquiris and piña coladas will add the bright color needed to add spark to the scene. Don't forget those little paper umbrellas to garnish the glasses.

For a more upscale menu just substitute filet mignon and seared salmon. The salads may remain the same or you might want to add a Greek salad with feta cheese. Remember people rarely remember what they ate at a party, only that they had a good time! The food should be secondary to the all-around theme of the event.

Make a splash with Baked Alaska for dessert. It is always safe to have fruit in case people are watching their weight. Watermelon would be perfect since it goes well with a barbecue.

After guests eat and mingle, begin with Wedding Bingo. You can order games by contacting bridalshowergamesAtoZ@gmail.com.

Opening gifts does not have to be boring anymore. Glitter rings may be passed out with the bingo boards (each one is different) and as the bride opens each present she will announce the gift and show the eager spectators. If the same gift appears in one of her squares she will cover the block with a ring. The first to have five across, down, or diagonal will yell "bingo" and win a prize. You would be surprised how this game breaks the ice and all families (friendly or not!) are now conversing: mostly about which square they need to win. But who cares, as long as they are not bored and are having fun. Prizes can be as simple or extravagant as your purse permits. Fancy jams, candles, scarves, nail polish, note paper, and movie passes are just a few ideas for your bag of loot for the winners.

If the title of your shower is BUY A GIFT AT THE BOUTIQUE FOR BETTY, then ask the guests to do just that before they come to the party. Tell them to spend twenty dollars (or any particular amount) and have the bride wear and display all of the items! If your title is Beth's Bridal Registry, bring one place setting of all of the china and silver and set up a small mock table with the place setting so that everyone can see what the bride has selected.

For Brenda's Bachelorette Weekend, plan for the bridal party to get manicures together. Open up lingerie at an intimate personal shower. Attend the theater together and talk…engage in friendly gossip…laugh and giggle with one another. Yes, it is okay to have the male stripper come. Why not?! Then go bar hopping at the hot spots in town. If the funds are available, rent a suite at a local hotel and slumber together for this fantastic weekend.

Present the bride with an album collecting old photos of all of you since you have known the bride. She will love the nostalgia and the fact that you have all changed (for the better of course)!

If you are using the title Bathing Beauty Bernadette, use beach towels and umbrellas for centerpieces. This party might be at the pool, at the local country club, at the beach, or indoors. For any passed hors d'oeuvres, use little plastic shovels instead of forks and serving spoons. Use paperback books, magazines, and suntan lotion for prizes. For place cards, fill small glasses with sand from the beach and put the card in the sand. If you really want to get outrageous ask everyone to dress for the beach. Another good gift for guests would be sunglasses. Remember, women like to dream and escape, so why not imaginatively take them away to Maui or Tahiti for a few hours.

If you want something extremely unique, use the "name in the sand" place cards. In order to accomplish this you will have to go to a beach when the sand is somewhat firm near the water's edge. With a stick or stem of a flower, write each guest's name in the sand. Then take a photograph of the name as the water is coming up on your writing. Do this for each first name. Develop the pictures and use these photos for place cards. If some of your friends have the same first name just put their last name printed on the back of the picture.

You can get these made if you would rather pay for this service. Leave plenty of lead time. The best way to distinguish tables at this party would be to use different flowers. For example, the first table might have violets as the centerpiece. When guests arrive have a long table with a small plant pot or pretty bowl (inside will be either Styrofoam or water) and place the eight or ten names of your friends sitting together at this table in the bowl. Use the plastic holders (to hold the sand pictures) that you can get at your local florist. The ends of the sticks will either be stuck in the Styrofoam or slipped right into the water. Once the cards are in place, cover the top of the plant pot with some violets. Repeat this same effort with Black-eyed Susans, mums, pansies, roses, lilies, daffodils, and so on. Of course each guest will take home her own sand picture.

INVITATION: A fantastic invitation for this party is a seashell that opens. Place all of the printed information about the party (place; date; time; RSVP) on a fancy piece of paper, fold it up, and place inside the shell. Mail the seashell in a box. Also, a message in a bottle is appropriate as an invitation. These objects may be purchased at local stores or online. You will need a lot of lead-time. Start planning at least four months in advance.

This party would lend itself to the Barbie-Q menu or use the Brunch for Betty menu and have the bash at 11:30 a.m. with bagels, lox, and cream cheese. Quiche Lorraine and French toast with flavorful syrups and cut up fresh fruit is also yummy. All of the other "B" titles may be interchanged and juggled with these innovative ideas. Also don't forget about balloons for this letter. There are all types of balloons nowadays with glitter and stuffed animals inside the center. Use these for decorations in the room or at the front door of the party location. It's festive and fun to decorate the bride's chair with fancy balloons.

3
"C" Parties

Champagne and Chocolate for Chloe

Congratulations Connie...We're Counting the Days!

CHERISH OUR CHER: COME ONE, COME ALL!

Carrie Caught the Bouquet!

Cookies, Cakes, and Caviar for Catherine

Celebrate with Charlene at the Club

Candles Shine for Corinne

Carol's China Pattern

Cindy Cries for Joy

Collect gifts for Colleen

Custom Collectibles for Chastity

Cocktails for Cameron

Choose Gifts Carefully for Charlotte

Certainly Celine Will Sing at the Shower

Cynthia's Crystal Sparkles

Creative Crafts for Cassie

Consequos for Consuela

CATCH CLARISSA'S BOUQUET

Caitlin is Like a China Doll

Crack Open the Bottle for Courtney

Colorful Collectibles for Chelsea

Calla Lilies For Camille

Crystal is Sparkling

Champagne and Chocolate for Chloe

There are many restaurants that offer a dessert bar that is perfect for this type of party. If you have your celebration at a private home, try to come up with as many chocolate desserts as possible. Some favorites: chocolate mousse; chocolate pudding with whipped cream; devil's food cake; chocolate covered strawberries; chocolate ice cream with hot fudge; chocolate coconut cake; chocolate cupcakes; chocolate ice box cookies dipped in melted Heath bar crunch candy bars. For a unique basket, or for the protein conscious, health-oriented guests, you could fill it with Balance bars with chocolate covers.

Besides the champagne, have hot chocolate available with Baileys Irish Cream. Chocolate ice cream sodas are the perfect top-off to this afternoon or evening function. You can buy chocolate covered plastic spoons that melt in the coffee when you stir your beverage. These would also be perfect for the seating cards: just tie the nametag to each spoon.

There are so many activities to spice up the dessert party: wedding bingo, advice cards, wedding word scramble, or craft-making. (Contact: bridalshowergamesAtoZ@gmail.com for games and templates.) This could be making napkin rings or learning napkin folding or flower decorating. Pottery and glass blowing are also good choices. Invite a professional to come to the party and do a demonstration. Prizes for all of the games are naturally big chocolate candy bars. Enhance the tables with dishes of chocolate covered cashews.

Most of the "C" titles can be mixed and matched with themes from this party. There are also chocolate shops that will custom make centerpieces like a big chocolate heart or the bride's name in chocolate for the table that holds place cards. Tootsie Rolls and little chocolate lollypops are also fun to have around the tables.

INVITATION: Send the printed information with some chocolates. Fancy bonbons are available at any candy shop, online, or you can use a regular candy bar.

If you decide on *Cynthia's Crystal Sparkles* as a theme, try to hire a person who makes crystal sing. You might try and find this type of entertainment through a local college or university. Perhaps a music teacher in the community would have a lead on this type of individual. By rubbing certain types of glass they produce sounds that form melodies. Rented crystal glassware for all courses would be a must at this party.

Centerpieces for the tables could be rented or borrowed. Swarovski Crystal has some perfect pieces like a crystal wedding cake, miniature champagne flutes, roses, and candlesticks. You might have someone actually come to do a demonstration on the cleaning of crystal.

Here is a crystal theme for a brunch of twelve people, for an intimate party for the bride:

Each of the crystal place settings represents a movie and guests have to guess the name of the movie. This type of contest stirs up a lot of creative juices and there is lots of opportunity for prizes. The first place setting is *Love Story* (use a heart crystal), *Grapes of Wrath* (crystal grapes), *Toy Story* (a crystal present), *Lady Sings the Blues* (female crystal), *The Poseidon Adventure* (a crystal fish), *Driving Miss Daisy* (crystal daisy), *Out of Africa* (crystal elephant), *Hawaii* (crystal seashell), *Cabaret* (crystal musical instrument), *Crouching Tiger Hidden Dragon* (crystal dragon), *Shakespeare in Love* (crystal book), and *The Neverending Story* (crystal unicorn).

Remember to go around and collect all of the crystal before you serve the food. Gifts for the bride may be crystal jewelry or crystal pieces.

A simple but beautiful brunch is bagels with lox and cream cheese, herring, white fish, blueberry blintz soufflé, kugel and fruit salad. Coffee, tea, brandy, and some orange juice with champagne for mimosas and you are set. For dessert, try some fancy cookies or coffee cake. No one will be worried about the food when they see your table so elegant and ornate.

Auntie Robin's Blueberry Blintz Soufflé

Ingredients:
12-16 frozen blintzes (look in the market at the kosher section)
1½ cups sour cream
5 eggs (beaten)
1 cup sugar
1½ tsp salt
3 tbsp orange juice
quarter cup + 2 tbsp butter

Directions:

1. Mix all ingredients and pour over frozen blintzes in an 18x24 baking pan.
2. Bake for one hour at 350°F.
3. Serve hot (10 – 14 people).

Creative Crafts for Cassie might be held at a pottery location. These enterprises are springing up all over the place. The guests pick out a piece to complete by painting and then firing in a kiln to keep or give to the bride. Some reputable pottery companies are also offering this at their manufacturing plants. This type of party would work well if you are going out later for the evening to meet the men at a bar or dance club. All of the showers can be Jack and Jill's—they are certainly not just for women. More and more parties are being planned with the groom and his friends as well.

For the party **Consequos for Consuela** contact bridalshowergamesAtoZ@gmail.com to order Bingo games and Advice & Recipe cards in Spanish as well as English.

4
"D" Parties

Dynamic Dancing with Deborah

DIAMONDS FOR DEENA

Donna's Dream House

Dress for Diane's Shower

Display Your Happiness for Darcie

Dawn's Drinking Day

Decorate Your Package for Drew

Dream with Daisy

Dearest Dee Decides to Dive into Marriage

Delightful Dining with Deirdre

Daniella is Divine

Dynamic Dancing with Deborah

Here's a party for the crowd with a lot of energy. Ballroom dancing, line dancing, swing dancing and square dancing are just a few of the various ideas you can use for a fun pre-bridal event with men and women. One main concern is finding an appropriate hall or facility that has enough room to spread out and where noise won't be an issue. Many of the dancers that you would hire for this type of entertainment already know the good places that will accommodate your guests. It might be a local YMCA, a house of worship, your country club, or even a campsite or park.

INVITATION: Send a CD. Music will give your guests the inspiration to get psyched for the party.

At *Dress for Diane's Shower*, naturally, the wardrobe will be mapped out if you plan to square dance. If it happens to be a fifties party with hula hoops the dress would be announced accordingly. You could title the party as Donna's Dream House and ask the guests to make her dreams come true with all of the objects and possessions that will create the perfect house.

Delightful Dining for Deirdre is very simple. Choose one of your favorite restaurants and plan the party in their private back room. If you have the funds just buy out the restaurant for the night and use the whole place. Some restaurants are closed on particular days—or at least one day a week; maybe you could convince the owner to open for your party on that day. You know the guests will be happy with the food if they all order right from the menu. Then you don't have problems with the picky eaters (there are always a few).

DIAMONDS FOR DEENA may be interwoven with any of the other parties. Have a gemologist come to the party to give a little demonstration and let everyone try on the gems. The girls will love this entertainment. Plus it's very educational. Just check with the reputable jewelry stores in your town or city. They will probably be able to arrange a demonstration, as it will be great publicity for their store. Or check with the groom to find out where he purchased the bride's diamond and ask that owner to help find a qualified gemologist. Great centerpieces for this party are different jewelry boxes, borrowed or rented. The guests can open the boxes and you could fill them with gifts for everyone to take home. Small pins or barrettes would be fun. Special cleaning cloths for silver or gems will probably be available from the invited speaker.

INVITATION: Buy jars of diamond cleaner at your nearby jewelry store and send this with the invitation. Your guests will be thrilled.

5
"E" Parties

Exciting Entertainment at Eve's Event

Elizabeth Will Express Her Excitement

Entice and Embellish Erin

Emma Embraces Love

Eclectic Gifts for Eileen

Ella's Extravaganza

Erica's Engaged

Emily's Elegant Event

Earth Colors for Eleanor

Elsa's Etched Smile

ELEGANT ELATED EDITH

Help Us Entertain Esther at the Shower

Eden Emits Love

Exciting Entertainment at Eve's Event

The key to a successful party is making sure the guests have a good time. Regardless of who attends—friends, relatives, neighbors, men, women or children—you want people to have fun, be relaxed and basically enjoy themselves. The way to accomplish this is have some sort of entertainment. That may be as simple as just having games for the guests to play (you will learn more in the category), having a hired professional (specifics to follow), or getting guests to participate in the event, such as dancing.

There are all kinds of people you can hire for entertainment: astrologer, artist, ballerina, caricaturist, cake decorator, drummer, entertainer, flower arranger, guitarist, handwriting analyst, ice sculptor, interior designer, jeweler, juggler, knitter, lingerie wholesaler, manicurist, napkin folder, origami expert, pianist, painter, palm reader, radio talk show host, singer, trio, underwear wholesaler, ventriloquist, violinist, wine connoisseur, xylophonist, yoga expert, zany clown.

Sometimes it's a good bet to start with the Internet and find something local to your city where you can hire someone. I know a terrific ice sculptor located in the Gloucester, Massachusetts area (he does travel) but it's not likely he will go to California for a shower. By researching professionals in their specific fields, you might get recommendations from friends or colleagues in other cities or from the web. Through a vast network you will eventually find what you need somewhere near your party venue.

Always ask for a few references and call the people who have hired the prospective entertainers. That way you are aware of what to expect and have discussed specific incidentals that you might have forgotten about. It really isn't necessary to hire the entertainer for a long period. Sometimes forty-five minutes is plenty. Remember there will be more things to do at the event, like eat, socialize, open gifts, and more.

Other forms of entertainment include guest participation. Group events like theater, miniature golf, going to the movies, bowling, carnival rides, playing croquet, kite flying, salon and spa visits may also be interwoven into your fun-packed party. Many of these ideas work well if you are planning a bachelorette weekend or a Jack & Jill shower (men and women). If the guest of honor happens to have a passion for a particular sport or musical instrument try to key in to her tastes. A Boston Red Sox game on the East Coast or an Angels or Dodgers game on the West Coast is a great way to bring two baseball-loving families together.

Remember, pre-bridal events, including rehearsal dinners and the brunches before the wedding should be light-hearted and entertaining. You are trying to bring people together who will now share a common bond (the bride and the groom), whether they have anything or nothing in common. It's quite tricky since you are usually dealing with several generations (from the flower girl to the great-grandmother) and individuals who may come from completely different backgrounds. That's why an activity is highly recommended—then your guests do not have to rely on too much dialogue.

Elsa's Etched Smile is a good title for your party if you are having an artist or a caricaturist as a part of the entertainment. Great prizes for this type of party when you play some bridal shower games might include colored chalk, artist's pencils, fancy crayons, monogrammed pens, or even sketchpads.

Earth Colors for Eleanor can create a gardening theme for

your party. You might use plants for centerpieces. For the seating arrangement, name each table a different color, like yellow ochre, burnt sienna, crimson, coral, beige, tan, caramel, and almost white. You can find these interesting color swatches at your local paint store, or Home Depot or Lowe's. Just type or write each guests name on their particular color and arrange the tags on those plastic stick holders you get at the flower shops. All of these can be stuck into a large Styrofoam ball that you put in a gorgeous vase. If you are really feeling creative, cut the color swatches into heart shapes or any other cool shape you like. A flower arranger would add just the right kind of entertainment to this party.

INVITATION: Send packages of seeds (for a flower or plant) with the printed info about the date and time of the event. Whenever you can think of an object to incorporate as part of the invitation, you have added another dimension to the event.

Ella's Extravaganza has a very special ring to it. Why not continue that theme throughout the party. Ball gowns or masquerade is a great possibility here. Send the invitation with an eye mask (with a stick on one side). Give out prizes for the most beautiful costume or gown, the most unusual, the funniest, the sexiest, the most coordinated. There is no limit to the categories you can come up with. Centerpieces might be different masks or objects from fairy tale heroes and heroines. You could use the famous glass slipper, a magic wand, a tiara, the shining armor, a king's cape, a crown, a jeweled necklace, a fancy mirror. Any sort of juggler, vocalist, puppeteer, and/or musician would be great entertainment for this extravaganza.

Name each table a different room in a house in the Eclectic Gifts for Eileen theme. Use foyer, guest room, pantry, sun porch, vestibule, dressing room, as well as the usual kitchen, dining room, living room, or den. For place cards, cut out a bold shape for each room, such as a large grandfather clock, a mirror, a sofa, a plant. Write the guest's name on the shape and display the name cards in a large interesting dollhouse (may be borrowed or rented). Place the cards in all of the particular rooms and let your friends poke through the house to find their respective place cards (that are now eclectic objects). You also might assign a room in the house for each guest to coordinate their gift for the bride. The natural entertainment at this party would be an interior decorator or a Feng shui specialist. Most people love to learn about easy and exciting design ideas, tricks, and ways to create beautiful rooms.

INVITATION: Send fabric swatches or paint color charts with the written information.

For Help Us Entertain Esther at the Shower bring in a lingerie or underwear wholesaler. Having each guest try on the scantiest, sexiest undergarments (can stick to nightclothes, for the modest at heart!) would be an absolute riot for the bride. Don't forget to have cameras ready and available for guests who may not have smart phones. Make a deal with the person you hire to use some of the products for prizes for your games. This party works best in a private home. Give a prize to the girl who makes up the best short story about her night in the outfit. Also, have prizes available for the best new title of the party, like "Naughty Nightie." Don't forget to have plenty of wine and champagne flowing at this event.

INVITATION: Send a thong in a colored envelope.

6

"F" Parties

Fern is Forever Fanciful

Find Faith a Fabulous Gift

Featuring Future Bride Flori

Fancy Fotos For Fran

Fondue For Frankie

FIONA FELL IN LOVE

For Friends of Florence

Fun with Francesca

Fabulous Faye

Life Will Be Fruitful for Francine

Fern is Forever Fanciful

This party is sure to be fun! Rent a cotton candy machine or an ice cream truck to be part of the day. Have candy apples like at a carnival stand and all sorts of fried dough and pretzels. Make it a true fanciful time from when guests can remember being a child. Send some interesting penny candy (button candy on long sheets of paper) as part of the invitation or even a bunch of Tootsie Rolls. Fill large sand pails with candy and goodies for the centerpieces. Or make each table a theme of a childhood activity, for instance one might be a kite, a bicycle, a pair of roller skates, balloons. Or you could name each table differently: Cotton Candy; Fried Dough; Candy Apple; Ice Cream Sundae.

Use lollipops for place cards. You can find the most elaborate at fancy candy shops, online, or just inexpensive, small ones at the supermarket. Attach each person's name to the stick or place it on the face of the lolly. You can make these on your computer or have a calligrapher come if you're planning a very fancy shindig.

INVITATION: If you would rather reverse these, you could send out lollipops with the invitation and save the button candy for nametags and place cards.

An entertaining activity that the bride will love for this theme involves childhood memories. Ask the guests to go around the room and tell something special she shared with the bride, way back when. There will be people at the event that just met the bride recently (from the other side). Ask those guests to imagine the bride as a character in a child's storybook—who would she be and why? This event lends itself well to an outdoor theme at a beautiful park or country club. It's even better if you can make it seem as though they are attending a real carnival.

If you can rent or buy toy Ferris wheels, they would be excellent centerpieces. Cut out photographs of the bride and groom (kissing; hugging; laughing) and mount and paste these cutouts in the seat of the Ferris wheel.

Enjoy *Fondue for Frankie* at an intimate party or a large bash. You will most likely have to rent or borrow a lot of fondue pots with forks. The beauty of this event is that you can have a successful party without having a sit down meal. Fondue is delicious and can be served and eaten in an informal, buffet style atmosphere. If you are cramped for space and can't seat thirty-plus people, this is a good solution.

Start with cheese fondue for the appetizers. Have meat and chicken for the main course and fruits and cakes with chocolate and caramel for dessert. Side dishes might include pasta, tossed or Caesar salads, or sliced veggies.

Here are the recipes.

Fondue Savoyard

Ingredients:
> 2½ pounds Gruyere cheese (or your favorite cheese) or half gruyere half Emmental (mixing cheeses is okay)
> 3 cloves of garlic
> 2 glasses dry white wine (8 ounces)

Pepper

Dry mustard (or paprika)

2 pounds French bread cut into squares

Before the Party:

1. Rub fondue pot with garlic (use use one clove).

2. Place about 6 ounces of wine and 2 remaining cloves in pot.

3. Warm slowly.

4. Add all of grated cheese.

5. Let cheese melt while turning with wooden spoon.

6. If too thick add more wine.

7. When creamy add pepper, pinch of dry ground mustard.

8. Fondue pot is ready to be placed on burner.

Chicken Fondue

Ingredients:

6 pounds chicken (cut in cubes)

Marinade (teriyaki, honey, or favorite salad dressing)

Olive Oil

The day before:

1. Place the marinated chicken in plastic bag in refrigerator.

2. Turn and shake a few times during the day.

Right before the party:

1. Heat oil in fondue pot.

2. Arrange raw chicken pieces on platter next to fondue pot.

3. You are ready to have guests cook.

May also be served with beef instead, or both, if you like.

Chocolate Fondue

Ingredients:
   1 cup cream
   1 pound semi sweet chocolate bits
   ½ cup of sugar
   1 tbsp butter
   1 tsp vanilla

Right before dessert:

1. Melt butter.

2. Add chocolate bits and stir until melted.

3. Blend in the sugar and cream (a little at a time).

4. Stir constantly until fully blended.

5. Add vanilla.

6. Serve on fondue burner with cut up fruits and cakes.

You may substitute chocolate bits for peanut butter bits or white chocolate bits, or have one of each.

The best type of entertainment at a fondue party is hand writing analysts, palm readers, or astrologers. Since the guests need to work with the entertainer one-on-one and rotate every ten or fifteen minutes, you want a buffet meal.

INVITATION: Send clips from a horoscope book or magazine. If you have any knowledge of the guest's sign, send the appropriate one, for example, Cancer for a June 22nd birthday. That may be difficult unless it is an intimate shower with a handful of guests.

7
"G" Parties

Greet Gwyneth…Play Games

Get to Know the Groom at Gretchen's Party

Guitar's Strum for Grace

Get Your Gift for Gail

Give a Gift to Gladys

GLORIA'S GODDESS PARTY

Gems for Gina

Gabriela Glows

Gardens Grow for Ginger

Goldi's Guests Gather

Generations Group for Geri

Georgia Gazes at the Gazebo

Greet Gwyneth…Play Games

Even though your guests aren't children, adults still love to play games. Especially if you are combining individuals of different ages and backgrounds. Very often, the bride has met a man who lives in a different location, maybe even across the country. Families may be meeting for the first time at the pre-bridal event. More than likely the parents have gotten together, but all of the aunts, cousins, and friends from the other side will be strangers. There is nothing better than bridal shower games to break the ice and help the guests to bond.

You have already read about playing Wedding Bingo (pages 13-14) at the party. Wedding Word Scramble is also a great game to be played during the meal (details to follow at "W"). For your invitation, send a few of the glitter rings from the Bingo game in your envelope. You can find these online or contact bridalshowergamesAtoZ@gmail.com (Spanish and Jewish versions available as well) and send one with each invitation. You can't imagine how much more exciting your event will seem if you send an object in the mail as part of your invitation. No matter which party you are having from the ideas in this book, the pens or glitter rings will be appropriate. For other ideas: send a pair of dice, a set of jacks with a ball, a playing card, pencils with the bride and groom's name printed on it, tic-tac-toe boards, or a jump rope.

INVITATION: Send a pair of dice with the invitation.

At *Get to Know the Groom at Gretchen's Party*, you can play The Newlywed Game. Have someone who is close to the groom (definitely make sure the person who makes the phone call has met the groom) telephone about a week before the party. The purpose of the call is to ask the groom some specific questions about his courtship. For example:

- **Where** were you when you first met?
- **What** was she wearing on your first date?
- **What** is her favorite song?
- **Where** were you when you first kissed her?
- **What** is her favorite movie? Perfume? Vacation spot?

Swear him to secrecy—he cannot tell the bride you called!

Write down all of his answers—verbatim! Then at the party, when the groom has arrived, start the game. You will ask the bride the same exact questions and ask her to tell you what the groom said—not necessarily what the real answers are, but what she *thinks* the groom said. People will be roaring with laughter. Before you start, if there are a total of fifteen (or any amount) questions, ask the guests to guess (and write on a piece of paper) how many the bride will answer correctly. Have prizes for the people who guessed the right number. Movie passes or gift cards for the local Dunkin' Donuts or ice cream shop are fun to hand out.

There are many group games for entertainment that may be combined at these parties. Miniature golf is fun if you are having a Jack & Jill shower. Also, croquet is great if you are having an outdoor event. The men love to play because they are so competitive. Horseshoes is another great possibility, or darts if you are inside. Form teams with two or three couples and have lots of prizes, for the first, second, third, and last places. Prizes for these events might be a backgammon set, traveling scrabble, cross-word puzzles, Sudoku books, or playing cards. If your shower is just women, consider Mahjong, and have Parcheesi, Rummy-Q, and Scrabble available for guests who don't know how to play Mahjong. A shower such as this should be scheduled for many more hours. A complete evening or afternoon will be needed. This type of party is great if you are on a limited food budget or you just want to serve munchies and dessert. A buffet is wise here because you won't have time for a sit down meal and all of the games.

INVITATION: Send sheet music for **Guitar's Strum for Grace**. You might choose the bride's favorite song. On the back of the sheet, print all of the party information. Naturally, the entertainment at this party would be a guitar player. Ideally you will find someone who can make up songs using the guests' names, with various verses. Use notes of the scale and G clefs for place cards. Have miniature or toy musical instruments as centerpieces or repeat various sheets of music on stands (with different songs). With the name of each guest, write the song so that they will find their tables by the names rather than by table numbers. Make sure the guitar player can play the song that was sent as the invitation.

For prizes at this party make or buy CDs for the guests. The grand prize might be a lesson with the guitar player. A good game to complement this party involves the groom. Have the guitar player strum some notes of a song that means something to the couple and have the bride guess where they were when they heard the song (same idea as the Newlywed Game but utilize music).

GLORIA'S GODDESS PARTY is ideal as a costume party. Guests should dress up as a goddess. If it is a Jack & Jill have them dress as gods & goddesses. The entertainment that fits here is an astrologer or a palm reader. Pieces of cut crystal are good centerpieces or a big crystal ball. Regardless of which menu you choose, have a large crystal punch bowl (may be rented if you can't borrow one) for the drinks. Crystal cups or glasses will be an added attraction here. Make ice cubes in the shapes of stars to float in the punch bowl. Color the ice or use orange juice or cranberry juice to form the ice pieces.

The ideal entertainment at a goddess party is an ice sculptor. Have him or her carve a goddess as you watch. Large bowls of grapes should be displayed everywhere—use every color you can find. Ask all of the guests to remain barefooted. If you really want to get crazy, organize a place where they can all dance on the grapes and squish them with their feet. Everyone will laugh and have a real ball. If you go this route, make sure you have a place for everyone to clean their feet with plenty of soap and fresh towels before they go home.

The coordinating prizes would be scarves, astrology books, and/or charts. For place cards, use names of famous gods and goddesses for your tables.

INVITATION: For the invitation send a halo or get some glitter that has stars and moons and put it inside the envelope. You could also send a magic wand.

Hire a gemologist for *Gems for Gina* for your entertainment. Have a lot of mirrors around so the guests can try on some of the fancy necklaces and watch each other modeling the goods. You might want to send a small pocket mirror as part of the invitation. Make sure to throw in a few glitter rings from the bingo game (to buy copies of the bingo game, contact bridalshowergamesAtoZ@ gmail.com). Since you are on the jewelry theme it will make more of an impact. If your party is Pearl is Our Pretty Woman (page 102) utilize these same ideas.

Name each table a different gemstone: diamonds; emeralds; rubies; pearls; opals. Find some costume jewelry that resembles each gem and drape it on a mirror as your centerpiece for each table. Other inexpensive little bracelets or rings made of shells or beads may be used as place cards. Just attach each person's name through the jewelry and display the hanging gems on a large cutout cardboard of a figure. You can attach the bracelets with thumbtacks or tape to the cardboard or Styrofoam. Write each guest's name on the large figure. Then place the piece of jewelry right next to their name. The prizes at a gem party might be pins, barrettes with stones, jewelry of any kind, ornate buckles for shoes, and fancy socks with little gems on them. This entertainment is also good for the GODDESS PARTY.

INVITATION: Send a handful of glitter rings with the printed info. You can get them off the internet or at a party store in your vicinity or contact bridalshowergamesAtoZ@gmail.com.

Also, you could use the ice sculptor for Gardens Grow for Ginger. He/she could carve a floral arrangement or a bouquet of flowers. And a must for a game at Ginger's party is guessing the spices. Have a table set up at a convenient place with open jars or dishes filled with various spices such as cumin, coriander, sage, paprika, and onion salt. Number each dish and give out cards to each guest. They should smell the spices then write the numbers and next to each name the spice. Collect the cards and check them and give out prizes for the winners. Buy some spices for gifts and wrap them with gift-wrap paper with foods printed on them. Other possibilities for prizes are potholders or salt and pepper shakers.

An alternative game that is similar if you are having a party for Heather, Rose, Iris, Violet, or Daisy involves flowers. Display a beautiful table with various flowers, you only need one of each so don't panic (it won't cost a fortune). Next to each flower write a number and ask guests to write out a card with the names of all of the flowers. Use unusual ones as well—not just tulips, roses, orchids, pansies, carnations—so everyone won't win. Give out prizes for the winners. Miniature vases, watering cans, plant pots, or baskets make great gifts for this party. Needless to say centerpieces would be flowers or plants. For variety make one table silk flowers and one glass blown flowers.

You could ask your local florist to come and demonstrate a flower arrangement for the group as part of the entertainment. There are also some creative people who can fold tissue paper into flowers —that's a good alternative as well. If you are definitely having an outdoor party, spice it up even more. Send the guests in teams of two on a bit of a "flower hunt" (more coordination for sure).

In order to guess the name of each flower, they will have to find the flower first. Give the guests clues all around the yard, country club, park, yacht club or wherever the party takes place. The fun part of a scavenger hunt here is making up clues that involve the bride.

For instance, if her name is Rose:

- *Clue #1 might be: Somewhere near the hammock you will find a flower that the bride is named for.*
- *Clue #2: In a hanging basket you will smell the bride's favorite flower.*
- *Clue #3: The first time he gave her a flower it was what color? (look around a window).*
- *Clue #4: His favorite outfit you wear with a floral print has _____ flowers (look near the porch).*

And so on.

These games are appropriate for *Hors D'oeuvres in Honor of Heather*, *We Value Violet's Friendship*, and I DO, I DO, IRIS SAID. **Rosie's Registry Rocks** would also be perfect with a gemologist—all upcoming.

Hiring a make-up artist for **Gabriela Glows** allows guests to watch a demonstration. For the game, add to the word scramble Bride and Groom, The Bride's Makeover or Geraldine's Makeover (substitute the name of your guest of honor). You will find details of the word scramble at the W party on page 133; to buy Scramble games contact bridalshowergamesAtoZ@gmail.com. Have all of the guests work on this game while the demonstration is taking place. You can have lit candles on various tables during this party.

Some ideas for prizes are candles, combs, beauty products,

make-up, and nail polish. Place cards could be small candle-holders with names attached.

INVITATION: As part of the invitation you could send a candle in a box.

8
"H" Parties

Hawaiian Honeymoon for Helene

Hearts of Love for Haley

HUNT UP a TREASURE FOR HOLLY

Hors d'oeuvres in Honor of Heather

HARPS PLAY FOR HOPE

Have Your Hair Done with Helen

An Heirloom Adorns Hillary

Hand Out Prizes at Hilda's Shower

Honey, Hugs for Helaine

Help Henrietta Celebrate

Harriet's House Party

A Husband for Hannah

Hawaiian Honeymoon for Helene

With a party focusing on a tropical island you have a built-in theme. Paper or flower leis are the perfect place card. Attach each guest's name to a lei and display them on a table with a Caribbean cloth. A private room at an Asian restaurant works quite well for this party. After making all of the arrangements, ask the restaurant for sets of chopsticks and use those to mail as part of the invitation. Prizes might be Caribbean cocktail napkins, fancy flowered scarves, or belts. You can also order Hawaiian grass skirts for guests to wear or use them to skirt the tables. Chinese lanterns would be an added attraction here as well.

Entertainment at this event might be hula dancers, fire-eaters, or musicians of any sort. Mix this up with some bridal shower games (email bridalshowergamesAtoZ@gmail.com for games) and your guests will feel like they have left their usual surroundings and have been transported to another island.

INVITATION: Send a map of Hawaii or some travel pamphlets.

Hand out Prizes at Hilda's Shower gives you a great opportunity to have guests win! Play tons of games at your event. Every aspect of the party can be a game. Hide clues all around the house: in the bathrooms, in the coat closet, on the porch, in the kitchen cabinets, anywhere that strikes your fancy. On the outside of a folded note write a message that says For our guest…Be sure to use pretty bridal paper (may be bought at your local wedding boutique, hobby store, big box store, or office supply store). On the inside of the note, direct the guest to open a drawer or look under a drape or under a sofa. At that location have a wrapped prize with a note that says,

"Congratulations—this is your prize" or "Congratulations—you have found your treasure," or "Celebrate! You have won!" You could leave another clue to have the guest go to another location in the house for their surprise. This is like a scavenger hunt. Prizes that would work need to be small—little candles, or jewelry, note paper, pens, goodies, nail polish, socks, soaps, and more.

This is a great party for **HUNT UP a TREaSURE FOR HOLLY** also. Have centerpieces that are treasure chests of one kind or another. Have them filled with costume jewelry (half opened). You can borrow from friends or buy some inexpensive beads.

This type of game requires planning ahead and placing all of the paper clues well in advance. You might need a helper to get this ready in time. It does provide a lot of fun and basically everyone likes to be a winner and take home a prize. Centerpieces at the tables should be the most outrageously wrapped presents stacked one on top of another. It's very easy to collect interesting shaped boxes or pick some up at different stores at the mall. A nice theme here is soft pastel colors. Have each table be a different color (pink; lilac; lime green; peach; cream). Wrap boxes in various textured paper and prints of the designated color. Place cards will be a tiny wrapped jewelry box (could be empty) with the same wrapping paper as the centerpiece on their table and a tag with guest's name. That is how guests would find their seats.

INVITATION: In the invitation place confetti that is shaped like little gift packages.

Have Your Hair Done with Helen is a perfect opportunity for the bridal party to bond. Plan an afternoon out together to visit a favorite salon. Have magazines, tea and coffee, and some treats available. What more can you ask? That is, besides some good gossip and a new hairstyle! This party works well also for manicures and pedicures. If the budget is unlimited why not go all the way with a day at the spa.

INVITATION: For this invitation, send a fancy comb, mirror, or brush in a little box.

Of course your theme for Hearts of Love for Haley will be hearts of all sorts. Even your food can be shaped into hearts. Cakes, cookies, and cupcakes are easy. Use the same heart molds for tuna fish salad, egg salad, chicken salad, and/or salmon salad. Make your gelatin molds in the shape of a heart. If you want to serve meat, make a great meat loaf or turkey loaf in a heart shape. Get some large Styrofoam hearts at the party or arts and crafts store. Stack these from largest to smallest in the center of your buffet table and cover with large tablecloth. You will now have a magnificent centerpiece in the shape of a large tiered heart. You can place foods in various dishes on these tiers. A nice prize or gift would be mugs that have been printed with a heart.

INVITATION: For the invitation, send a heart-shaped candy box and put the information on the inside printed on a heart, of course. Ask guests to dress in red or wear something red to the party. For the charitable crowd use this theme for donations. If the bride does not need or want any gifts, all of the guests may make a contribution to the Heart Fund. This is a perfect party for donating to charity. It's also fine to interchange the name and use Hearts of Love for Lenore or whatever the bride's name is.

9
"I" Parties

Ivanka Is the Icing on the Cake

An Ivory Party for Irene

I Love You Cards for Isabella

I DO I DO, IRIS SAID

Ilsa Invites You to Celebrate Her Love

INTERIORS FOR IVY

Inspiration for Izzy

IDA INSPIRES LOVE

An Interesting Invitation for Ilyse

Ideas for Irma's Interiors

INNOVATIVE INGRID

I'm In Tune With Ixia

Ivanka Is the Icing on the Cake

This is the perfect party to have a cake decorating specialist as the entertainment for your event. For fun you might want to have the party at a bakery so that everyone can make a small cake and learn some decorating techniques. You could also incorporate cupcakes or cookies using different shapes. If this party is going to be at a restaurant, place cards may be various cake recipes on fancy paper rolled in a scroll. Attach guests name on the outside of the scroll with a fancy ribbon. Table centerpieces could be a canister filled with sugar, flour, or brown sugar. Other choices may be a sack filled with peanut butter and Nestle chocolate bits. Just mix and match all of the ingredients of baked goods and display them in interesting containers. Prizes for any games played should be baking utensils, potholders, or aprons.

INVITATION: With the invitation, you could send cookie cutters in different shapes such as lips, hearts, or flowers. This works well with the party titled *An Interesting Invitation for Ilyse*. A key element to a successful invitation is planning an interesting stamp. Check out what is available at your local post office. If a love theme is not in stock try to match your theme or the color scheme to an appropriate stamp. You may have to order stamps from one of the main offices to get what you like. It's worth researching because everyone will notice your attention to detail.

INTERIORS FOR IVY or **Ideas for Irma's Interiors** would be an exciting party with an interior designer. Ask guests to bring gifts for one particular room in the house. Maybe you could divide the guest list into fourths and have some bring presents for the kitchen others for the bedroom and some for the den or bathroom.

INVITATION: Incorporate the following poems with your invitation:

Ivy will need assistance and aid
In the kitchen where meals are made
Bring a gift that she would find
Go to her kitchen registry, everything's outlined.

Iris is a romantic at heart
Think bedroom, and be smart
When you're shopping for gifts for her
Think texture like lace, satin, or fur.

Isabella is so practical, we know
Choose a gift for the den, like a throw
Or go to her registry and find
Something that is one of a kind!

The bathroom will be Irma's delight
Everything will look just right
Choose a gift for this room in her place
Think outrageous to fill the space!

Inspiration for Izzy is the perfect party to have an astrologer, palm reader, or handwriting analyst. When the bridesmaids and maid of honor are getting together for a girls' weekend, this kind of program can be a lot of fun. It is more intimate and there is more time to spend with the hired professional.

10
"J" Parties

Jean Will Juggle Her Gifts

Jane Can't Wait…Just Three Months 'til the Date

Juggle Jewish Word Scramble with Julia

Just Bring Yourself to Celebrate With Jamie

Juliette Opens the Jewelry Box

JOIN US FOR JODIE'S EVENT

Janice Joins the Love Machine

Jennifer's Shower Features Jewish Wedding Bingo

Jacqueline Jumps for Joy

Jaden's Jazzy Shower

Join Joyce in July and Party...Party...Party!

Jill Joins the Couples Craze

Julianna's Joy

Janet Jets Around the Globe

JUBILANT JUDITH IN JULY

Justice of the Peace for Jessica

Jasmine Jams

Join Jerri in June

Just for Jocelyn

Jean Will Juggle Her Gifts

What a terrific idea to have a party with a carnival theme. Jugglers can provide the entertainment either at the individual tables (roaming) or at a designated stage. Find out ahead of time what props the jugglers will be using. For instance, if they say knives, use this item as one of the centerpieces. Perhaps you could give the guests ideas such as unfilled salt and pepper shakers, wooden spoons, and the like. Other carnival ideas that may be incorporated would be toy Ferris wheels with pictures of the bride and groom in the seats (also mentioned in an earlier party, page 40). Make sure to take pictures when the bride is taking a quick lesson on how to juggle.

A fun game with this party for guests is to have everyone write a message to the bride about *Juggling Life as a Wife* on postcards that are sent in advance with the invitations. They are similar to the recipe and advice cards that may be ordered online or contact bridalshowergamesAtoZ@gmail.com for cards. At the party, read some out loud and see if the bride can guess who wrote the card.

Centerpieces may be playful: a toy seesaw; a toy convertible; a swing set; a bicycle built for two. The idea is juggling real life with fantasy and play.

INVITATION: A cool picture of the bride and groom during their courtship at a carnival or juggling with bowling pins. You will have to stage this in advance or Photoshop it.

Jacqueline Jumps for Joy also lends itself to these carnival themes. Centerpieces could be a jump rope folded up and belts folded the same way. You might even want to have a hula hoop contest at this party. Another possibility: CDs with music from Tae Bo or Zumba, with an energetic flow. You could use these for prizes.

At 𝕵𝖆𝖓𝖊𝖙 𝕵𝖊𝖙𝖘 𝕬𝖗𝖔𝖚𝖓𝖉 𝖙𝖍𝖊 𝕲𝖑𝖔𝖇𝖊 your theme will be places around the world that the newlywed couple wants to visit. Keep that theme going when guests arrive at the hotel or restaurant. All of the table place cards may be attached to some luggage in the foyer or lobby. Write the name of the guest and the name of the country where they will sit. Decorate each table with a flag from the country or a poster from a travel company. Try to coordinate gifts for guests. For instance, at Britain have some English tea bags. For Mexico have some miniature sombreros. China may have some rice cakes or chopsticks. Italy will be perfect with some interestingly shaped pasta. Berets would be in order at France. Passport case holders may be ordered online and they make great prizes for your bridal games.

INVITATION: Send luggage tags (from the airlines) as part of your invitation.

For **Jaden's Jazzy Shower** ask guests to bring something for the bride that would be considered jazzy. It could be something she might wear, something in which she might dress her future husband, or something she may use in her house. Decorate tables with a miniature shower that is jazzy. This will take some creative planning and several trips to Home Depot or Lowe's. You might make one that is all beaded. And one that is mirrored and one with drinks attached to the inside. Just have fun and let loose. A faux painter would be fun entertainment at this party to demonstrate some jazzy techniques on wall samples and let guests try a few-like marbling, wood graining, or glazing.

Join Joyce in July and Party...Party...Party This
party should definitely take place at a beach or a pool. You may use a private home or a country club, whatever is available. There are many public beaches in various cities throughout the country. If there is not a food stand available for buying the meal, just bring coolers and have sandwiches or salads. Trust me: the food will not be the prominent part of this event. Lots of suntan lotion, big beach towels and blankets, and girl talk is all you need. Have a manicurist come and do everyone's polish on their fingers and toes. Give gifts of nail polish and sunglasses. This is a great party if you are on a strict budget.

INVITATION: Send sunglasses or suntan lotion as part of the invite.

Jennifer's Shower Features Jewish Wedding Bingo, "thank heavens," says the grandmother of the bride! She's very happy her granddaughter is marrying a boy who had his Bar Mitzvah when he was thirteen. This customized game is fun to play when the bride is opening her gifts. For Jewish bridal games contact bridalshowergamesAtoZ@gmail.com. No one is bored and they all love to win at bingo. Have some great prizes available; there are many ideas throughout the book. You can play this game anywhere—you don't have to be sitting at a table. The cards will fit pretty easily on your lap if you are crammed for space.

"Oy vey, we're playing *Juggle Jewish Word Scramble with Julia* at the shower." Yes, Grammy, we are! And the customized bride & groom pencils come with the game. "Thank God!"

It's a lot of fun to ask your guests to bring a mechanical gift (something that resembles a machine or is plugged in) to *Janice Joins the Love Machine*. For entertainment invite a salesperson who can demonstrate a new electrical item either for the kitchen or bathroom, or even a cool recliner. If you would like the party to be more craft-oriented, you could have supplies from an art store and ask the guests to build a new love machine. This event will require space and long tables with items that include glue, scissors, string, and pieces of wood.

In preparation for a party such as this, ask your guests to rent and watch the movie *Honey, I Shrunk the Kids*. This will work best if you have a small group and the guests are hands on and creative.

INVITATION: Better yet, send the DVD of that film as the invitation.

If you have a big budget, mail your invitation for *Juliette Opens the Jewelry Box* in a box. Find a chic velvet jewelry pouch online, then fold the printed portion of the information inside and mail this as your invitation for the party. You can print the text on your own computer but make sure to use fancy paper from an office store. Also, order well in advance since you need extra time for this type of preparation. Prizes for any games should be jewelry, of course.

INVITATION: Jewelry (costume is fine) or the jewelry pouch.

A gemologist is the perfect entertainment for this party. A fancy mirror at each table will be the centerpiece. Hang one strand of pearls or a locket on the edge of the mirror for an added touch for this party. Place cards should be small boxes wrapped with feminine paper. The box may be empty or inside may be the number of the table where the guest will be requested to sit.

For the party, *Join Jerri in June*, since pearls are the June birthstone, you can carry over the gemologist theme mentioned above. Your guests can guess what everyone's birthstone is depending on the month they were born. Have a prize for the guest who gets the most right—a jewelry item, of course.

11
"K" Parties

Kendra Confirms This Is Love

Keepsakes for Katherine

KATIE WILL KISS THE GROOM

Kerry's Kitchen Registry

Keep the Date for Kimberly's Shower

Kisses and Hugs for Kelly

Karla Counts the Days

Yeah! Kathy Caught the Bouquet!

KRISTEN KNOWS THIS IS IT!

The Countdown for Katrina

Karen's Continued Kindness

Kendra Confirms This Is Love

Planning this shower for Kendra involves movies with the theme of love! This makes a great slumber party or weekend away for the girls, either at a house or hotel. *A Man and A Woman, Love Story, Out of Africa, The Unsinkable Molly Brown, Pretty Woman, Love Affair* (to name a few), are some ideal choices. Plan a brunch or deli lunch with a lot of pick-up foods and with all of your movie rentals, just hang out. Have some wine and beer handy. Gifts for the bride-to-be may be items that the bride would wear when feeling amorous! Some natural ideas are lingerie, sexy nightclothes, fabulous perfumes and bubble baths, luxurious towels and bed sheets—satin or monogrammed for extra pampering.

INVITATION: Send a movie that has to do with LOVE!

Kerry's Kitchen Registry is an ideal party with a cooking theme. Some stores that sell kitchen appliances offer cooking classes, which would be an excellent idea for this shower. If you want to have your party at a private home, you could invite a guest chef to teach a cooking class for your guests. It's fun to arrange your meal around the food you will be preparing. There are various options and it is best to discuss the choices with the restaurant or country club where you will be having the class. For the invitation, be sure to send recipe cards to all guests. They are available at stationary stores, or online or contact bridalshowergamesAtoZ@gmail.com. Prizes for games at this shower could be measuring spoons, potholders, and oven mitts—anything used in the kitchen. Centerpieces will look and smell great if you use spices. You can decorate the bottles or jars with colored tulle bows. With a bigger budget, you can use canisters and fill them with various types of pasta or cookies.

INVITATION: Send a large wooden cooking spoon or fork with the party information attached.

At a shower with the theme Keepsakes for Katherine, it is fun to ask your guests to relay a special time they shared with the bride. Ask the guests to bring an item or keepsake (it could be a photograph) that will remind her of that event or moment. Find an interesting box to keep all of the items in. For photos, display them in a special album that the bride will cherish forever.

You will have to do some legwork in preparation for **KATIE WILL KISS THE GROOM**. Ask the bride's mother, sister, friend (anyone you can think of) to give you some interesting photographs of the bride and groom kissing at different places. Now you see why this will take some serious work in advance. You may even have to set some of this up (without them knowing of course) in advance. Take these photos and enlarge them to 8x10s and use them for the centerpieces at the various tables. Choose basic frames or even borrow some from relatives or friends. During the party ask guests at each table to start a story about the couple with clues from the picture at their table. Each guest should say two or three sentences then the next person continues from there. Have prizes for the most fantastic story, the most realistic story, and the funniest story. The bride may have to be the judge here. Prizes could be as simple as a unique box filled with Hershey Kisses or kissing bears that may be purchased online or at a supermarket.

INVITATION: In the envelope add some Hershey Kisses.

12
"L" Parties

Lights ... Camera ... Action ... Linda's in the Spotlight!

Luscious Lingerie for Lisa

Lorraine's Luncheon !!! Come one, Come all

Laurie's New Love

LINENS FOR LUCY

Lights Shine for Lenore

Lindsey Lights up the London Club

Look Up Recipes for Louise

Learn About Cooking at Lilly's Shower

Links for Lauren's Friendship

LYNN'S LAVISH LUNCHEON

Ladies, Let's Party at Leslie's Shower

Light Up Your Life, Lola!

LOVE LAURA'S SHOWER

Listen to Music at Lany's Shower

Lights ... Camera ... Action ... Linda's in the Spotlight!

This is an ideal time to have a fashion show for your guests. There are many small boutique shops that are willing to come with their clothes and put on a fashion show for a bridal shower. Just research the stores in your area if you would like to have this kind of party. For lots of fun, have the bride dress up in a casual outfit, then an everyday outfit, and at the end of the show an evening gown. She will absolutely have a ball. Choose a place for the shower where you will have some privacy and plenty of space for the models to change. You may need to have it at a country club or a private room in a restaurant if you are not using someone's home.

Centerpieces might be handbags or mirrors. You could have each table be a different color. Select the handbag in the color of the table. If your guest is sitting at the red table, use swatches of fabric (red in this case) to be attached to the place cards. If a guest has a yellow fabric swatch she will find the centerpiece that has a yellow handbag. Try to coordinate the same color napkins as well. All tablecloths may be white or cream. If you can't find or afford colored cloth napkins, buy some colored tulle and tie a bow (with the appropriate color) around the white napkins. Have plenty of cameras available to take pictures when the bride is modeling.

Any menu will be perfect at this party. You can be as simple with just desserts and coffee or have a full course meal, depending on your budget. If you know the bride's favorite color, place her at that table.

INVITATION: Send a scarf, handkerchief, hat, or gloves (something you wear) with the written information. Use a fancy box. Use the computer or if you have good handwriting, or want to hire a calligrapher, handwrite the title of the party with a fancy font (different examples are in this book) and cover the box with the paper that has the title **Lights … Camera … Action … Linda's in the Spotlight!** on it.

For a party with the theme *Light Up Your Life, Lola!*, cameras are a must. This shower can be a lot of fun by photographing the bride with different groups at the party. Set up categories. For instance, you might call up the names of everyone there who is related to the guest of honor. Then take photos; do an actual photo shoot. Call everyone who went to the same college as the bride. Have some props (the graduation yearbook). Have a category for anyone who works with Lola. Again, bring some things representative from the office for the shoot. Next, ask everyone who has a birthday in the same month as the bride. Have a calendar on hand and find the month of the bride's birthday. Ask them to pose silly; serious; high society; thoughtful. Another good category is anyone who has traveled with the guest of honor. Bring some passports and little suitcases for props.

Some of the groups will be very small—two to three people. And some will be rather large—perhaps six to ten people. Here is a list of other categories from which you may choose:

> *Guests who are the same age*
> *Guests who went to the same high school or middle school*
> *Guests who live within a 30-mile radius*

Guests who went to the same camp

Guests who will be related from the other side

Guests who are single

Guests who are married

Guests who are grandmothers

Guests who have traveled abroad

Guests who were in the same sorority

Guests who are teachers

Guests who work on charities

This becomes a lot of fun if you can move the photo shoots around to different areas of the party. For instance, if you can go outdoors and be by a beautiful tree or a pond. Have some of the groups pose around the car—coming out of the doors. Use different rooms of the house or club (depending on where the party is). Think up as many props as possible and bring them in labeled bags or boxes so that you will be able to find them at the right time.

Another way to experience this event and make it lots of fun is to list the names of the guests in a particular category and ask them to guess what they all have in common with the bride. Have prizes for the person who guesses first. Small photo albums or frames would be excellent gifts.

Since you will be getting up a lot and moving around at this event, a buffet works well, either for brunch or lunch. You could have an omelet station or a crepe station going, and a fantastic fruit and vegetable table so that guests can munch while they are waiting to be photographed. For dessert, have crepes, bananas foster, or cherries jubilee—always yummy and festive.

INVITATION: Mail a roll of film with the invitation. As technology has changed and film has gone the way of VHS tapes and AM/FM radios, you may have to search online but it's still available. By nature of its antiquity, it's even more of a conversation piece and will get the invitation noticed! If you prefer to send something extravagant, choose a picture frame and put a picture of the guest of honor in it or the printed information about the party. If you can find a custom chocolate house ask them to make a camera in white or dark chocolate and send this as part of the invitation or wrap them up for favors to give to each guest as they leave the party.

Look Up Recipes for Louise has the same possibilities as the party *Kerry's Kitchen Registry* Have a guest chef for *Learn About Cooking* at *Lilly's Shower* or invite the author of a good cookbook—giving away copies of the book, which you have purchased, as gifts for each guest.

Lindsey Lights up the London Club can only take place in NYC or Los Angeles since that is where the London Club has its hotels. They have a superb tea with sandwiches and pastries for a set price per person. It's all about elegant surroundings from the first moment and a beautiful private room.

13
"M" Parties

Mamma Mia, Molly's Getting Married!

Marriage Tips for Meghan

A Marvelous Menu for Mary's shower

Meredith's Marriage Will be Monumental

Make a Page for Maggie

MANICURES WITH MICHELLE

A Movie Marathon With Melanie

Marvel at Melissa's Love

Music and Merriment for Monika

Meet the Groom at Marilyn's Shower

Miraculous Marsha Melts With Love

Mihaela's Make-Up Party

Marian Marries...oy...The "Mishpacha"

Make a Date in March for Melody's Shower

Thoroughly Modern Millie Will Marry

Make a Package for Maria

MINDY AND ME

Martha Matters

Mazel Tov Miriam

Meet Meg at Menopause The Musical

Mamma Mia, Molly's Getting Married!

What a perfect time to have a party at the theater. The show Mamma Mia is so vibrant and exciting, or **Meet Meg at Menopause The Musical** for a girls getaway to Harrah's Hotel & Casino, Las Vegas (go to www.menopausethemusical.com); your guests will never forget this event. You will have to secure tickets well in advance (look for a group rate) and check out what cities have these plays available. *Thoroughly Modern Millie Will Marry* also is a perfect theater party. Bring snack bags with goodies and treats for your guests. Buy them drinks at intermission and believe me they will be talking about your shower for a long time.

INVITATION: If you want to be outrageous send the CD with the invitation so they will be familiar with the music. No one will miss your party. Theater glasses or baby binoculars are also good choices to send with the printed information.

Mihaela's Make-up Party can be a blast if you plan it just before everyone has a big night out on the town. Invite a make-up artist to come for a demonstration. She could do a little bit on everyone or just a complete makeover on a few guests. You could decide depending on your wallet and the time factor. Have some tropical drinks and wine available and hot hors d'oeuvres. A dessert bar with make your own sundaes and cookies will be perfect. The highlight of this event is the make-up so guests will not be looking for a full course meal. For prizes for bingo and other bridal games use some of the make-up products that your entertainer will probably be selling. This is also a fun party to have at a salon when they are not open to the public (Sunday or Monday).

INVITATION: Send a tube of lipstick or nail polish with the information about the party.

Miraculous Marsha Melts With Love deserves an ice carving for the entertainment. There are some splendid ice carvers who can do some exciting demonstrations. This party works very well outdoors at a pool, on a deck, either at a home or country club. You could carry over the melting theme with baked Alaska as the dessert and hot tuna melt sandwiches. Don't forget melted marshmallows in s'mores (graham crackers, chocolate Hershey squares, and toasted marshmallows in a sandwich). If you have additional funds hire a snow cone machine vendor to make snow cones before they melt! Ask the ice carver to provide centerpieces: perhaps an ice carved heart. At a pool party they will melt from the sun to add to the ambient theme. If you would prefer an evening event, try a séance with a fortuneteller, which goes well with candles galore flickering on your tables.

INVITATION: Send an ice cube replica that lights up and flashes when you drop it in your drink (may be found in novelty stores or on the Internet). Or you could send a candle with this invitation. On the back of the envelope of the printed information, melt some wax and put an imprint with a heart or a flower to enhance the melting theme.

You must play the Newlywed Game at Meet the Groom at Marilyn's Shower. This game is described in detail in the

"G" party (page 48): *Get to Know the Groom at Gretchen's Party.* There are so many possibilities for **Music and Merriment for Monika.** A guitar player, a singer, a trio or a harpsichord player are just a few choices for your entertainment. There are also some great folk dances, square dances, and line dances that would be fun at this party. Just make sure you have enough room at the location you select. As a courtesy, take music decibel levels into account so as not to disturb the neighbors.

INVITATION: Send sheet music, perhaps from a favorite song of the bride-to-be, or a song that was popular when the couple met or got engaged. A small musical instrument like a harmonica or a set of baby maracas or a tambourine would be fun as part of the invite package (you may interchange this with *Listen to Music at Lindsay's Shower*).

A Movie Marathon With Melanie is the perfect party for bridesmaids on a weekend away. Rent a lot of wedding movies like *Goodbye Columbus, The Wedding Planner,* and *Father of the Bride.* Then show love-oriented movies such as *Romeo and Juliet, Shakespeare in Love,* or *Two Weeks' Notice.* Huge bags of popcorn and pretzels and lots of liquid–wine or soft drinks, hot chocolate, and cider are vital to have on hand.

This party may also be used with MANICURES WITH MICHELLE. You could all give each other manicures or plan to go together to a salon with simultaneous appointments. Better yet, arrange with the owner for teas and treats—perhaps to take over a portion of the salon or hold the event on a Sunday when it is typically closed. Naturally you'll have to pay salon staff. Many times an owner is all too happy to comply as it boosts exposure for the establishment.

INVITATION: Send a pink bottle of nail polish with this poem:

We're having a movie marathon
So what does that have in common
With manicures and polish so pink
The perfect party—so what do you think?

Come to celebrate Michelle's shower
At two o'clock, that is the hour
Meet at the Bliss Salon, 6 French Street
You'll feel like you're at the Plaza Suite!

Then a sleepover we've arranged for us all
With lots of popcorn—you're sure to have a ball
Marvel at the bride's love while you give her a marriage tip
The champagne and wine will flow—have another sip!

Underlined words may be interchanged depending on the details of your specific dates and places.

The **MINDY AND ME** theme may be incorporated with many of the other parties. When you invite the guests ask them to come up with two items that go together like peanut butter and jelly, and why that is like their relationship with the guest of honor (because they were inseparable while growing up in grade school). Another example might be the chicken and the egg, because we could never figure out who would go first. This game works well at a sleep over party when everyone is pretty silly and guests have had a few drinks.

INVITATION: Send a photo clip of things or people that go together, like Lucy and Desi, Tarzan and Jane, Cleopatra and Antony, Sonny and Cher, sun and moon, salt and pepper, toothpaste and toothbrush, champagne and caviar, peanut butter and jelly, pillow and blanket, milk and cookies, and more.

14
"N" Parties

News Flash: Nancy's Getting Married

Notice Natalie's ROCK

Nice New Clothing for Nicole's Shower

Negligees for Noreen

NEWLYWED NINA

Noteworthy Event! Nora's Bridal Shower

Noisemakers for Nelda

Nanette's Night

Naomi as a Newlywed

Notice Natasha

News Flash: Nancy's Getting Married

As soon as your guests arrive, before they even enter the main door, have a photographer snapping pictures—in the style of a newspaper photographer. Centerpieces for this event can remain newsworthy. Create a newspaper clipping of the engaged couple in exotic places such as South Africa, Croatia, Tahiti, or Austria with an interesting story. Frame these news clippings and stand them up in the center of each table. You could drape a single red rose or white orchid beside the frame. This will add the romance and softness to the newspaper print.

Use postcards from different vacation spots for place cards. Each table will represent a unique place and have a different card. Write a clever note, for example:

> News Flash...about your space
> Have a seat and take your place
> At table eight
> Don't be late!

Repeat the first two lines on all of the postcards and change the verse for the numbers, for example:

> Go to number one
> To start the fun!
>
> You're at table two
> Enjoy the brew!
>
> This is your afternoon spree
> Meet us at table number three.

You're at table four
With drinks galore!

Feeling perky and alive
Meet us at table number five.

Number six means half a dozen
Join us there and meet Nancy's cousin.

Please be seated at table number seven
The food is delicious; you'll be in heaven!

A candle will shine
At your table number nine

You won't see any men
At your table number ten.

Underlined words should be changed depending on the guest of honor's name.

INVITATION: Sending an invitation in the form of the front page of a newspaper will stir up excitement for your party. Try to incorporate a photo of the engaged couple if possible. Use your local print store or the Internet to help you create the text and make authentic copies. Mail the newspaper in a colored large envelope. These may be purchased at Staples or a FedEx store locally in your town. You will need to start planning this kind of program many months in advance.

Negligee's for Noreen deserves a naughty-nightie party theme. Have a sales person from a lingerie store (or a particular clothing line) come with samples and stock so that everyone can try on the goods. You might want to add slippers or robes also. If you have a small group of people like the bridal party, maybe have the event at a store like Victoria's Secret or Lady Grace after you check with the manager in advance.

When guests have on their nightgowns, ask them to describe their ideal night when they model the clothes. Make up some funny and cute stories to go along with the fantasies. Whatever you do, don't forget to photograph it.

INVITATION: Send a pair of panty hose or bikini underwear, or some night cream with this poem:

Do you wear a nightshirt, negligee, or sleep in the nude?
We invite you to try on samples and exude...
On celebration of Noreen's big day
You'll fantasize and frolic in a romantic way!

Size: Whatever fits
Style: Whatever fancies
Fabric: Whatever feels good

An intimate shower
Meet us at Victoria's Secret at four
Try on black, red, pink, and more

Underlined words should be changed for your specific party.

At the party **Noisemakers for Nelda,** use interesting centerpieces that represent musical notes. For instance, one table would be a drum, a trumpet, a violin, a flute, a guitar, and bongo drums. (Borrow or rent the instruments.) Prizes for all games at this shower could be CDs. Photocopy sheet music from the bride's favorite songs for place cards. If the violin table is the theme from Titanic, have that same sheet music in the center of that table. Write each guests name at the top of the page of the same music, that is how they will find their seats at the right tables. Place a large table in the center of a foyer with a vase of flowers. Then stagger the sheet music in a circle around the vase in alphabetical order by names. If you have a larger budget, harmonicas and/or maracas would be great prizes or favors also.

INVITATION: Send a CD with the invitation. Or record the invitation and have the information be played to the guest on a tape.

Notice Natalie's ROCK should have a gemologist as the entertainment. Have all of the girls' rings cleaned at this party. The speaker can bring the equipment and do this very easily during the party.

15
"O" Parties

Once Upon a Time Olivia Fell in Love

OPEN GIFTS WITH OPRAH

Opulence at Olive's Shower

OPALS FOR OPHELIA

One Man for Odessa

Once Upon a Time Olivia Fell in Love

Begin your invitation with *Once Upon a Time there was a little girl…* and keep this theme throughout your shower. Ask each guest to bring a little story about an experience with the bride. When guests share their special time with the guest of honor, have them begin with the same phrase, *Once Upon a Time…*It could be a comical moment, a treasured time, or a specific event they shared such as a graduation, prom, or sales promotion at work. Because this title lends itself to fairy tales and books, have the bride sitting in a special chair that has been decorated lavishly. Use books for centerpieces. They could be borrowed or secured at a local library.

Have different themes at each table:

- *Once Upon a Time there was a kitchen…*Use recipe books here.
- *Once Upon a Time Olivia fell in love…*Use poetry and love books at this table.
- *Once Upon a Time there was a king and queen who traveled…* Use travel books from another country at this table.
- *Once Upon a Time there was a mystery…*Thrillers are stacked at this table.
- *Once Upon a Time there was a contest…*Sports books are perfect at this table (the groom won't feel left out).

By the way, this is a great theme for your rehearsal dinner or a party when there are men and women.

Prizes for games should be small pocket books or paperbacks, instead of the usual seating cards. Use your computer and some very elegant fonts to create a large page for each table. Start the page with *Once Upon a Time there was a kitchen...*and then list all of the people that will be sitting at that table. Use a different font for each table. Recreate that title at the table and guests will find their places very easily. If you have a good-size budget, buy all of the books and give out the centerpieces. Either ask the guests at each table who has the closest birthday to the date of Olivia's wedding date, or place a bookmark under one of the dinner plates at each table, and when the guests find the bookmark say the winner of the centerpiece is sitting to the right (or left) of that person. The guest standing with the bookmark keeps the bookmark.

INVITATION: Send a little book of one sort or another. There are some very interesting small books. Have the text with information begin with *Once Upon a Time...*or send a bookmark.

OPEN GIFTS WITH OPRAH is a party that should have Wedding Bingo (pages 13-14). After you buy the game you could send each guest a bingo board as part of the invitation. Contact bridalshowergamesAtoZ@gmail.com to buy Bingo games in either English, Spanish or Jewish versions..

INVITATION: Use the following poem with the bingo board you send (change the underlined words to fit your specific party):

Please bring this card to Oprah's shower
Saturday, May tenth at two, the fun will begin
Bingo! As Oprah opens her gifts—you could Win!

Underlined words may be interchanged for your specifics.

Opulence at Olive's Shower is exactly that. Be prepared to spend a lot of money if you're going for a theme like this. This is a decadent party with all of the frills. Start with custom designed invitations from BK Designs: www.bkinvitesu.com ($$$$). The invitation is always an object; it could even be a personalized board game. You can see many examples and possibilities of this creative work on the site.

Whether you're having an elite caterer or going to the finest restaurant or country club, plan fabulous foods. The time of day or night you choose for the party will determine the type of menu you select. If the theme is sushi/Asian, have the chef create a spectacular dessert. A Chinese take-out box in white chocolate filled with raspberries and ice cream (mango or pistachio) coming out of the box; chopsticks should be made of dark chocolate. Your guests will rave.

At an opulent party, everyone should receive a gift. Edible, colored ice cubes are the newest craze. You can buy them (with a name imprinted on them if you want to be extravagant) from the Internet. They look like ordinary ice cubes, but when they are placed in a drink they light up different colors and they glow. Very hot! Pack come in threes, sixes or twelves depending on how much you want to spend. Your guests definitely will not forget your shower. Leave plenty of time for imprinting, so order early (at least six weeks is recommended).

16
"P" Parties

A Progressive Party for Polly

Put a Poem on your Page for Priscilla

PREPARE A RECIPE FOR PERRI

Picture Paula Prepping to be a Bride

Penny Will Be a Princess at Her Wedding

Pick Out a Gift for Pam

Play Wedding Bingo at Pat's Shower

Pearl is Our Pretty Woman

Play a Tune for Peggy

A Pottery Party for Penelope's Shower

Photographs for Phyllis or Flowers for Phyllis

Your Presence is Patricia's Present

A Progressive Party for Polly

This is an ideal shower to have at three different houses if there are a few friends getting together to host the parties. The first will be for hors d'oeuvres, the second for the entrée, and the last dessert; if the houses are near enough so guests can walk from one to another, all the better. But, in case of inclement weather or distance, no problem, as this party is still successful even if you have to drive from place to place. If the gifts will be opened at the last house, have a decorated vehicle parked out front at the first house and collect the presents there so they can all be driven over to house number three. If you are living in a cold climate and guests will have coats, arrange for someone to bring them upstairs and lay them on the beds in other rooms of the house. It's unlikely that anyone will have enough closet space for forty-plus extra coats.

This party may be a weekend afternoon event or scheduled for early evening around 5 p.m. As guests arrive, have wine and beverages set up with little tags on the bottom of the glasses. Just rent glassware if you don't have enough. Small, dainty, bite size pizzas may be passed around. Crudités and cheese trays on coffee tables and some sushi will do the trick for your first course.

Have a Bridal Word Scramble game for the activity at the first part of the event (contact bridalshowergamesAtoZ@gmail.com for Word Scramble games). This will help break the ice and get everybody involved. Spend about an hour and a half or so at the first house. Then start moving everyone to the next location. You will spend about an hour and forty-five minutes at the entrée house. If you have helpers in the kitchen for serving, have them move with the guests as well.

Vegetable lasagna and lemon chicken with green beans and fruit compote is an easy, healthy meal. Rent dishes if you don't have enough china between all of the hostesses. Serve buffet style and have a large table set up with drinks and plain and bubbly water. Your guests will be rejuvenated. There's something psychological about going to new surroundings and starting over. It's almost like a new night. Also, the crowd moves around so people are talking to different guests and mingling more. At the second house, while everyone is eating, read some of the advice cards. Ask the bride to guess if the advice was written by a married or a single woman. You could also read recipe cards.

Then you are onto location number three. Here you will serve coffee, tea, dessert, and maybe have a champagne toast. Ice cream cake, fresh fruit, tarts, and pudding cups in chocolate dishes will top off the evening. Play Wedding Bingo (pages 13-14) as the bride opens her gifts. Have someone display all of the gifts at this house long before you arrive. This is a great way to spend a fun-filled, exciting shower. No one gets bored because they have so much stimulation from the different surroundings.

Be sure to include maps and addresses of all of your locations with your invitation. Perhaps you could have balloons out front at the mailboxes or at the corners of the streets. Try to make it like "follow the yellow brick road."

At **Play a Tune for Peggy**, why not have minstrels or singers? This party most definitely deserves entertainment from the music world. A guitar player or harpsichordist may also be good possibilities.

If you are interested in the party Photographs for Phyllis ask your guests to bring along some photographs and have them meet at a stamp store. They are cropping up in all cities and at the shopping malls. The party actually takes place at this business venue. Guests will make a photo album either to keep or give to the bride. You could bring in sandwiches or pick up pastries or do the entertainment, then go to a restaurant nearby. You will be limited on numbers with this event so check and see how many people they can accommodate. This might be a fun activity for just the bridal party.

If your party is centered around the slogan Your Presence is Patricia's Present, have some items representing charities available for guests to make a donation. They may want to send a card in your honor and that would be a generous way to help others. There are a multitude of organizations such as the American Cancer Society, Muscular Dystrophy Association, the Humane Society of the US, The National Runaway Safeline, Make-A-Wish Foundation, and local charities, to name a few. There are some folks who really do not want gifts for whatever reason and they choose to have donations made instead.

If you are having a party titled Put a Poem on your Page for Priscilla, ask your guests to write a page in a book. Collect all of the pages before the party begins and compile a scrapbook for the bride. It's always a good idea to send the pages to your guests so that the pages will look uniform. Ask them to be creative and add photos with their generous words. This will be a treasure when finished that the guest of honor will cherish. Prizes for any games could be poetry books.

Play Wedding Bingo at Pat's Shower.
The perfect entertainment at any bridal shower, regardless of your crowd, ages of the guests, different economic backgrounds, or gender, this game works (contact bridalshowergamesAtoZ@gmail.com for games). Everyone has a ball and believe it or not people like to win! When the guest of honor opens her presents she will show the gift and everyone will check their bingo cards to see if the present is listed on one of their squares. There are adorable packages of jelly rings that you can buy to cover the squares on the Bingo cards. Have lots of prizes: candy bars, candles, jewelry, perfume, and plants. After the first win, across, diagonal, or vertical, keep the card going to form a W or a T or an M, for example, then cover the whole card. You can have a lot of fun with this one. No one will be bored and everyone will stay until the end.

17
"Q"

Quality is Always Better than Quantity

Regardless of what time of day your party is, where it takes place, or how many people will be in attendance, quality is imperative. That means the food, the place, the gifts, the entertainment, the games and the invitation—everything involved with your event. People remember good things, but they don't necessarily remember quantities of things. It is more important to have one good dish rather than several mediocre choices. A spectacular dessert that tastes impeccable will make more of an impact than a huge selection of ordinary, everyday desserts. If you can only afford one game, make sure it is presented well and looks classy, rather than buying a lot of junky five and dime games. If you can only afford wine or one type of fancy drink, make sure it tastes wonderful. A big selection of common drinks will not give you the quality you're after.

Guests will definitely remember if they had a good time. That is why the entertainment and interaction part of your shower is so important. It's always a good idea to live by the phrase, "less is more." Just make sure whatever you are using: buying, renting, or borrowing, is of the highest quality. You won't be sorry. The same holds true for presents or favors for your guests. Whatever the budget (one dollar or one hundred dollars per person and everything in between), choosing a high-end product with a reputation for excellence is the way to go. In this case it might be a chocolate bonbon from Godiva that costs one dollar. On the high end you might choose a product from Victoria's Secret. Make sure your packaging and wrapping is fancy. Again, you must think quality, quality, and more quality!

18
"R" Parties

Raise Your Glasses for Robin

Roberta Will Rave about the Restaurant

Rosie's Registry Rocks

Remember a Time You Shared with Rhoda

Write a Recipe for Rachel

Receive Kisses and Hugs From Rena

Reeetas for Raquel

Ruby's Ring is Hot

Radiant Rebecca

Rita Renews her Wedding Vows

Reply Yes for Randy's Shower

Remembering Ravishing Rosalie

Let's Rendezvous with Roni

Let's Get Real With Renee

Raise Your Glasses for Robin

About three months before your party, contact some of your local liquor stores to arrange for a wine tasting event. They will put you in touch with the sales people that represent the wine companies and give you some choices as to who you can hire. This party may take place at a private home or at a country club or clubhouse in an apartment complex. The entertainer, a sommelier, will bring pamphlets and information about the various wines. Simple finger foods or hors d'oeuvres and a dessert table are sufficient for this type of gathering. You can ask guests to make a toast to the bride as you sample the different wines.

INVITATION: Find an invitation in the shape of a wine glass. Information may be printed on the front and back of the cut out shape. For added fun place a drink recipe in the invitation.

If your guest of honor has a favorite restaurant, splurge on **Roberta Will Rave About the Restaurant**. For Ruby's Ring is Hot and **Rosie's Registry Rocks**, have a gemologist come to entertain at these parties. In **Receive Kisses and Hugs From Rena**, have Hershey kisses everywhere for snacks and decorations. Have the group write down all of the places the bride and groom have kissed—the location, day, time, etc. Any details they can offer will help. Have the bride then read the answers and see who has the most right on the list; they of course, will win the prize.

Aim for a private room or at least a segregated section so that your guests will be set apart from the regular clientele for the night. Ask the chef to prepare your bride-to-be's favorite dish.

Add some bridal games and open gifts and Roberta will be very happy. It might be fun to have part of the meal prepared at the table. For example, a Caesar salad or crepes might be an excellent choice.

For the party **Reeetaſ for Raquel** contact bridalshowergamesAtoZ@gmail.com to order recipe and advice cards in Spanish.

19
"S" Parties

Shop 'Til You Drop For Samantha

A Sexy Stripper Stuns Us at Sofia's Shower

A Shopping Spree for Sally

Surround Susan with Champagne and S'mores

Save the Date for Sarah's Soiree

The Secret's Out…Sabrina's Engaged!

Scarlett is Simply Elegant - Come See!

Scramble Wedding Words at Sheila's Shower

Send a Reply for Stacey's Celebration

Sharon Shares Marriage Advice

SUE'S SPLENDID SHOWER SUNDAY

Share Your Recipes with Shelley Saturday

Sasha's Sushi Party

Smile with Stephanie at her Bridal Shower

Spring Is In the Air and Shannon Is Swept Off Her Feet

A Sophisticated Shindig for Sherry

Show Sandra Your Love at the Shower

A STAMP PARTY FOR SYLVIA

Simple and Stylish for Suzie

Shop 'Til You Drop For Samantha

This shower is an all-day affair. Meet at one house and break up into small groups of four to six women. Assign each group a different mall or shopping center. Give each team a list, like a scavenger hunt, but this will be a shopping spree. They will have to buy certain items for the bride—perhaps a negligee, a scarf, a T-shirt, a piece of jewelry, something sexy, something that smells good—you get the picture! The list can be as simple or as extravagant as you like. Ask your guests to chip in a certain amount of money and let them know in advance what that amount will be.

Give each group a few hours for shopping and then meet back at a designated house, restaurant, or club house for the party portion of the event. At this shower, when the bride opens the presents there will be explanations as to why the items were purchased and there will be many humorous stories about the day's escapades. It will be interesting to see if all of the groups pick similar items or all different. Of course keep all gift receipts in case there are duplicates. Eat comfort food at this party as everyone will be tired from all of the shopping! This party may also be used to plan, **A Shopping Spree for Sally** or *Simple and Stylish for Suzie* (both are mentioned in the "S" parties list).

INVITATION: Send your party information on a purse, large or small (depending on your budget). There are some very cute invitations on the market in the shape of a handbag and this will put everyone in the mood for a shopping spree.

20
"T" Parties

TRACE TANYA'S TERRIFIC LOVE LIFE

Tina's Trousseau Full of Treasures

A Toast for Terrific Bride Tracey

A Theater Party for Thelma

Te Quiero Teresa

Together We'll Treat Tristan

A Tiara for Tiffany

Shop at Tiffany's for Tammy

Tamara's Trust and Love

Tips of the Trade for Terri

Tabatha Talks the Walk: Down the Aisle

Taylor Will Be Touched

TRACE TANYA'S TERRIFIC LOVE LIFE

This party will be a little bit like a scavenger hunt with teams, depending on how many guests will be included in the shower. You will need to have some inside information about the groom and also where the couple first met and other adventures they have had together. We recommend at least three in a group and you can have as many as eight or so on each team. This party would also work well for a bachelorette weekend. Have bags ready with some pens, paper, and a map. Some of the clues you can include would be:

FIND: A cocktail napkin from a restaurant or bar at which the couple dines.

FIND: A candle that is the color of Tanya's outfit when the two first met (insert future spouse's name).

FIND: A photograph of one of the family members of the groom.

FIND: A receipt for something the couple purchased together.

TAKE: A picture of the location where the bride and groom worked out.

TAKE: A picture of the location where the groom gets his car washed.

DESCRIBE: The location of the bride and groom's first date.

FIND: A bottle of wine that the bride considers her favorite.

FIND: The book that the groom has read in the last six months.

FIND: Four selections of music that will be played at the wedding.

Feel free to add others or enhance this list in any way. The guest of honor will be allowed to answer two specific questions to each team privately. Also, there is a cap on money to be spent; the teams should not be allowed to spend more than forty dollars. So they will have to use their ingenuity in a lot of cases or beg, borrow or steal, so to speak. Since there will be a lot of logistics in this party and a lot of moving around it might be fun to all end up at a favorite restaurant or bar and order off the menu for the food part of the event.

For the party A Tiara for Tiffany have the bride try on various head pieces and veils and have everyone vote for their favorite.

21
"U" Parties

OUR UNUSUAL UMA

Unis is United with Uri

Ursula Understands Marriage

Youthful Uta

Ultima is the Ultimate

Ursa is Under the Sea

Unique Unice

OUR UNUSUAL UMA

Unusual is the name of the game at this party. Ask your guests to wear unusual clothes and to bring an unusual gift. Have all of the people who attend talk about how they came up with the idea for their unsual wardrobe. Serve unusual combinations of food—something the guests would not expect. This is a party to completely go wild! Anything GOES!

22
"V" Parties

Vanessa's Full of Vim and Vigor

Vivacious Vivian

Very, Very, Veronica

Vibrant Vicky in Voile

We Value Violet's Friendship

VOILÀ VICTORIA WITH A VEIL

Verna's Wedding Vows

Vanessa's Full of Vim and Vigor

Today's obsession of health and fitness is perfect for this theme. A glorious hike up Runyon Canyon or Griffith Park (in LA) or a beautiful spot in your hometown can kick off this party. Another possibility is to bring in a trainer from a local boutique health club like Barry's Bootcamp (in Boston, Chicago, LA, Miami, Nashville, NYC, San Diego, SF) to do a session in a large room or at the gym (prearranged, of course). Fancy milkshakes, smoothies, or other inventive health drinks after the workout will be enjoyed and appreciated. Share stories about the bride and how you all know each other. You may be able to get gift cards or work-out clothes for gifts for your guests.

After the workout part of this party take eveyone to Greenleaf Gourmet Chopshop, a healthy restaurant where guests can enjoy the most amazing salads. There is one across from Barry's Bootcamp, Hollywood and also right down the street from Barry's Venice, CA. If you are searching for other Greenleaf locations for catering a party on the west coast there are two in Beverly Hills, CA, one in Glendale, CA and two in Costa Mesa, CA. This is a health-oriented eatery offering made-to-order salads, wraps & sandwiches, plus a creative juice bar.The food is fresh and fabulous.

INVITATION: Have the trainer make you a CD of the music that will be used and send that with the details of the date, time, and place. Remember to let everyone know about the workout clothes they should wear.

For **VOiLà ViCtOriA LLitH a VEiL,** invite a hair stylist to play around with hair styles for the bride while the bride models her veil. Ask the guests to bring or wear something made of tulle (or lace) since the veil is most likely made out of one of those fabrics. Share your objects during the party. Discuss what the bride will bring or wear for her something old, something new, something borrowed, and something blue. Maybe she will pick something she sees at the party from a friend to incorporate in her special day.

INVITATION:

> *Let's all watch Victoria model her veil,*
> *Yes, just us girls, not even one male!*
> *You are invited to the bridal shower Saturday,*
> *   April 16th at two,*
> *Something old, something new, something borrowed,*
> *   something blue.*
> *We'll all help with this tradition*
> *To show our bride how it's done!*

Underlined words may be substituted and changed for your particular party.

On the table for the buffet have four sections, use very old dishes (borrow if you have to) for the appetizers or munchies. Use new, modern serving dishes and cutlery for the salads and use borrowed serving pieces (all mismatched) for the main dishes. When it comes to dessert just use all blue serving dishes or blue paper plates and plastic blue forks and spoons.

Menu
Pita and humus

Sliced, cut vegetables with onion dip

Cheese and crackers

Millionaires' salad

Greek Salad

Skewered chicken kabobs

Skewered meat kabobs with grilled vegetables

Tofu

Rice

Dessert Menu
Tarts covered with blueberries

Blueberry ice cream

Here is the recipe for the salad.

Millionaires' salad

Ingredients:
2 cups miniature marshmallows
1 cup flaked sweet coconut
2 cans mandarin oranges (11 oz. drained)
1 can crushed pineapple (20 oz. drained)
1 (8 oz.) carton low-fat sour cream

Directions:
Combine all ingredients and cover and chill.

23
"W" Parties

Winona in White

Wendy's Wild Wedding

Wilma the Wonder Woman

Whitney Welcomes Your Wishes

Play Wedding Word Scramble at Wanda's Shower

Winona in White

Your party will be all white! Here is an opportunity to have a party where everyone wears white clothes and all of the foods served are white. So much fun! White Dover sole (or swordfish) and white rice are the main dishes with cauliflower for the vegetable. Serve white cheeses for appetizers with white crackers or white bread cut in unusual shapes. Also, white hard boiled eggs sliced in half (yellow carved out and thrown away) sprinkled with a bit of salt and pepper. Try to use white dishes and white linens. Hopefully you can borrow them or the caterer or restaurant will have white. White candles of all shapes and sizes should adorn the tables and white flowers of every kind will be the centerpieces including lilies, orchids, daisies, and roses. Each table can feature a different white flower in glass vases.

Serve white-looking piña coladas for drinks or White Russians or white wine, as well as cream soda with vanilla ice cream floating in it. Have dishes of white marshmallows around and bars of white chocolates for extras. Dessert will be white coconut cream cake. Serve eggnog if you can find it, though it's not always in season, as it has an off-white color. A nice idea is to have white snow cones with amaretto or other after dinner liqueurs dripped on them.

Ask your guests to bring a gift that is gift wrapped only in white. Give a prize for the most beautiful looking gift-wrapped white gift (have everyone vote when all the packages are displayed). Also have people vote on the best white outfit, the most comfortable white outfit, the fanciest white outfit, the most unusual white outfit, the most casual white outfit, and of course the prizes will be white!! Some gift ideas for prizes are fancy white soaps, fancy white stationery, white gloves, white sun glasses, bath products in white jars.

A fun invitation is a bottle of white nail polish in a small white box mailed with a note that says:

> *White is pure*
> *Winona is excited for SURE!*
> *(Join us (date and time) wearing only white*
> *At (location); it will be a great night!*

For your party **Play Wedding Word Scramble at Wanda's Shower**, you can order some great games by contacting bridalshowergamesAtoZ@ gmail.com. Besides word scramble in English and Spanish, there are wedding bingo games and recipe and advice cards, also everything is available with a Jewish theme.

24
"X"

X-citing, X-cellent, X-traordinary

These are the main three words that you want your guests to use to describe your party/shower/event. Let's face it, years later no one ever remembers what they ate or what they wore, or what the weather was, or whom they sat next to. But they definitely will remember if it was an extraordinary time, and if they had fun and left feeling happy!

Everyone strives for excellence: When you look good, you feel good. When you dine out you want excellent service, it makes the meal. When you buy a new dress you want excellent manu-facturing and excellent designing. There's no end to our high expectations for vacations, babysitters, contractors, the book we just read, our children's grades, and the list goes on and on. So why should entertaining be any different? You should concentrate on a great theme so your unique party will be extraordinary. Keep it lively, fresh, exciting, and above all make sure everything you include is excellent—in every sense of the word!!

By incorporating a few of the hundreds and hundreds of suggestions and ideas on all of these pages, you will definitely be providing your guests with the ultimate bridal shower/party/ event that was planned X-plicitly for them.

25
"Y" Parties

Yes, Yolanda Said Yes!

What Will Yvette Get?

Youthful Yasmine

Yvonne is Your Bride

Yes, Yolanda Said Yes!

Si! Cain! Oui! Find yes words in other languages like the above in Spanish, Hebrew, French. This is a party that is positive and fun and fanciful. The web site www.blacklaceskinjewelry.com has a variety of what looks like decadent tattoos for your hands, arms, necks, shoulders, ankles, etc. Give each guest some of the products and ask them to come up with a variety of places to exhibit the fun skin jewelry; then have a mini fashion show (with music) wearing the adornments and seeing everyone's selections. Any of the menus from the other pages will work at this party or just do a dessert theme or a tea.

Tell the guests: "Yes, you look great." "Yes, you have A NEW LOOK." "Yes, we love you." "Yes, anything is possible." This is a positive motivational theme!

26
"Z" Parties

Zesty Zoë

Zero in on Zelda

Zsa Zsa

Zesty Zoë

For some real hot zest for this party, if you have an unlimited budget, book your group into the Venetian Hotel in Las Vegas. Take the gondola rides during the afternoon and visit Madame Tussauds Wax Museum right on the property. There are fabulous restaurants in what is a replica of St. Marks Square and they are always playing outdoor concerts there while you dine. There is no end to the shopping that is available at this hotel and many others along the strip. Be sure to have your camera and takes lots of pictures of the bride in "Venice." The live entertainment changes monthly so check the papers and the Internet if you would like to go all out and see a show in the evening.

For those of you who are on a strict budget, Zesty Zoë may be as simple as a shower in a home. Have all of the guests bring an apron and they will be divided into different groups to do the cooking and learn a few recipes, zesty ones for sure.

Grammy's Meatballs

Ingredients:
>   2 lbs. ground sirloin or ground turkey meat
>   1 egg
>   Bread crumbs
>   1 tbsp of ketchup
>   1 bottle of chili sauce
>   6 oz. grape jelly
>   2 tbsp hot water

Directions:

> Combine chili sauce, grape jelly, and water in a saucepan on the stove. After the meat is mixed with egg and bread crumbs, form small meatballs and place them into the sauce. Cover and heat for 45 minutes on the stove. Remove cover and simmer for 25 minutes on low flame. Stir meatballs now and then. Cook some white rice as a side dish.

For the *Zsa Zsa* party, have everyone dress up as their favorite actress. Of course some people will come as Zsa Zsa Gabor!

INVITATION:

> *For this party you will come*
> *As an actor from movies or TV*
> *Sunday June 2nd to have some fun*
> *Arrive in your outfit at three*
> *We'll guess who you are*
> *Because we know you are a star*
> *And here to celebrate our beloved Zsa Zsa!*

Please note that you would change what's underlined to fit your party!

And now you have an arsenal of ideas

Begin planning

Combine

Delve

Elaborate

Finesse

Go for it!

Helping friends have fun

Is the ultimate reward

Juggle the names and parties

Keep the ideas flowing

Learn to improvise

Mix and match

Notes from various pages

Or just follow the plan of one party

Picture a tremendous success

Quality counts

Reality comes from dreams

So start now

*T*his book will be your bible

*U*se family and friends to help

*V*iew a spectacle to remember

*W*ith love and heart

*X*pand your horizons

*Y*ou will be the greatest hostess

*Z*ero in on your plan and most of all…ENJOY YOURSELF!

COMING UP NEXT WILL BE

PARTIES
GALORE
and more
AZ

With More Than 220 Occasions and Themes

CPSIA information can be obtained
at www.ICGtesting.com
Printed in the USA
FSOW04n1653101217
42025FS